**This book is dedicated
to the people who like ketchup
on just about everything**

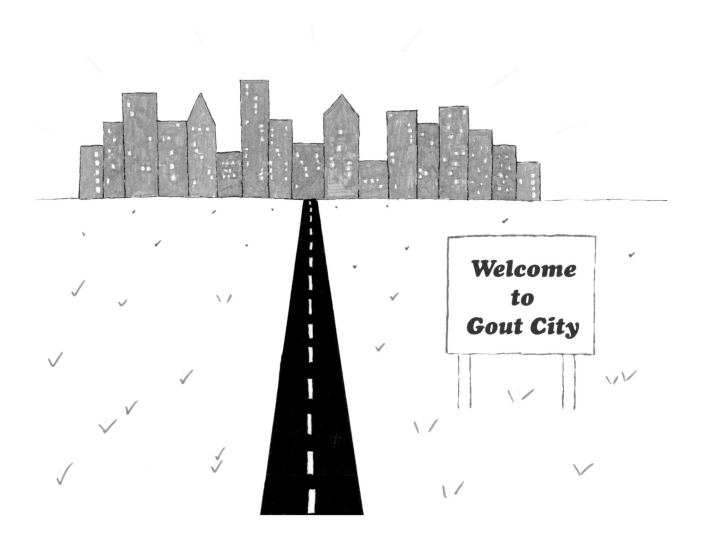

There once was a day
in the city of Gout,
a day to remember
because the ketchup ran out.

MENU

Scrambled Eggs............. $1.²⁵

Homefries..... .95¢

Fried Egg Sandwich...... $1.³⁵

Steak & Eggs... $7.²⁵

Porkroll Sandwich... $2.²⁵

Cof. Sorry

Toas

C'UP Sauce for Life

All over town
no one knew what to do,
when the ketchup, the ketchup
came off the menu.

The man with the ketchup
had run out of luck...

Out on the highway
in a broken down truck.

So when the stores opened,
on October the 12th,
not a bottle of ketchup
was left on the shelf.

Now this caused a panic
at everyone's table,
because food without ketchup
makes eating unstable!

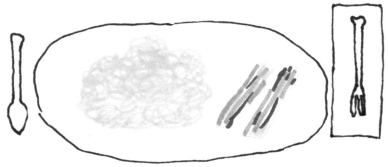

It started at breakfast
all over town,
whoever got eggs
just made a big frown.

"No," cried the people,
as they all started to pout,
"We can't eat these eggs
if the ketchup's run out.

The same was the story
at the diner for lunch,
you never did see
an unhappier bunch!

No one could swallow
their fish sticks or fries,
to all of their credit
not one person tried.

And eating a burger
was completely no fun,
since no one had ketchup
to place on the bun.

Far worse were the children
in all schools alike -
staring down at their food,
they all called for a strike!

No ketchup for nuggets
or patties of meat
gave children the reason
to simply not eat.

Dinner time came,
but the meal was a bust,
Mom's cooking in truth
kind of tasted like dust.

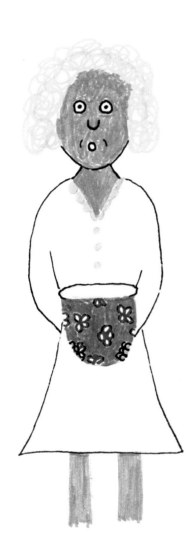
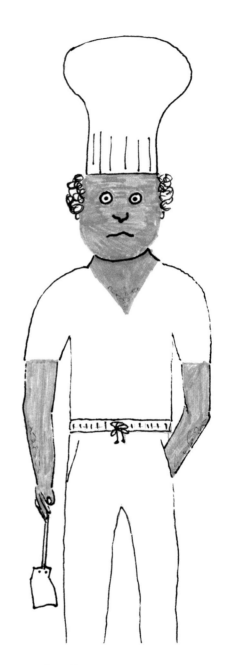

And that day...
   Every Mom - Every chef
     learned a lesson by heart:
If you don't have some ketchup
the meal cannot start!!

So OH! How they cheered,
nearly cried with relief,
when the ketchup-man showed
on October, 13th.

So if you want to know,
what this tale is about;
A word to the wise,
DON'T let the ketchup run out!

Order this book online at www.trafford.com
or email orders@trafford.com

Most Trafford titles are also available at major online book retailers.

 www.trafford.com

North America & international
toll-free: 844-688-6899 (USA & Canada)
fax: 812 355 4082

Our mission is to efficiently provide the world's finest, most comprehensive book publishing service, enabling every author to experience success. To find out how to publish your book, your way, and have it available worldwide, visit us online at www.trafford.com

ISBN: 978-1-4120-7220-5 (sc)

Print information available on the last page.

Trafford rev.04/09/2020

Printed in the United States
by Baker & Taylor Publisher Services